Mentoring

How to Develop Successful Mentor Behaviors

Third Edition

Gordon F. Shea

A Fifty-Minute™ Series Book

This Fifty-Minute™ book is designed to be "read with a pencil." It is an excellent workbook for self-study as well as classroom learning. All material is copyright-protected and cannot be duplicated without permission from the publisher. *Therefore, be sure to order a copy for every training participant by contacting:*

CRISP.
Learning
Menlo Park, California

1-800-442-7477

CrispLearning.com

Mentoring

How to Develop Successful Mentor Behaviors

Third Edition

Gordon F. Shea

CREDITS:
Senior Editor: **Debbie Woodbury**
Assistant Editor: **Genevieve Del Rosario**
Editor: **Brenda Pittsley**
Production Manager: **Judy Petry**
Design: **Nicole Phillips**
Production Artist: **Zach Hooker**
Cartoonist: **Ralph Mapson**

© 1992, 1997, 2002 Crisp Publications, Inc.
Printed in the United States of America by Von Hoffmann Graphics, Inc.

CrispLearning.com

02 03 04 10 9 8 7 6 5 4 3

Library of Congress Catalog Card Number 2001093514
Gordon F. Shea
Mentoring, Third Edition
ISBN 1-56052-642-4

Learning Objectives For:

MENTORING

The objectives for *Mentoring, Third Edition* are listed below. They have been developed to guide you, the reader, to the core issues covered in this book.

THE OBJECTIVES OF THIS BOOK ARE:

☐ 1) To explain how anyone can assist in the development of other people through mentoring

☐ 2) To suggest mentoring behaviors to adopt or avoid

☐ 3) To show how mentoring works in today's workplace

ASSESSING YOUR PROGRESS

In addition to the learning objectives, Crisp Learning has developed an **assessment** that covers the fundamental information presented in this book. A 25-item, multiple-choice and true-false questionnaire allows the reader to evaluate his or her comprehension of the subject matter. To learn how to obtain a copy of this assessment, please call **1-800-442-7477** and ask to speak with a Customer Service Representative.

Assessments should not be used in any employee selection process.

About the Author

Gordon F. Shea is the author of 15 books and over 200 articles on such subjects as organizational development, leadership/management, communications, team building, and workforce development. He enjoys an active consulting and training practice in those subjects.

Mr. Shea has authored a companion Crisp *Fifty-Minute*™ book for mentees titled *Making the Most of Being Mentored*. He has published dozens of articles on mentoring in such periodicals as the *Managing Diversity Newsletter, Supervision, Women in Computing, Bottom Line Business*, and the *Commandant's Bulletin* (U.S. Coast Guard).

Mr. Shea and Crisp Publications have also collaborated on creating a bestselling training video, *Mentoring*, which demonstrates both sides of the relationship.

Mr. Shea's Management Briefing book, *Mentoring: Helping Employees Reach Their Full Potential*, was published by the American Management Association for their membership list. This work is currently being revised and expanded for publication by Crisp Publications in 2002.

How to Use This Book

This *Fifty-Minute*™ *Series Book* is a unique, user-friendly product. As you read through the material, you will quickly experience the interactive nature of the book. There are numerous exercises, real-world case studies, and examples that invite your opinion, as well as checklists, tips, and concise summaries that reinforce your understanding of the concepts presented.

A Crisp Learning *Fifty-Minute*™ *Book* can be used in variety of ways. Individual self-study is one of the most common. However, many organizations use *Fifty-Minute* books for pre-study before a classroom training session. Other organizations use the books as a part of a system-wide learning program—supported by video and other media based on the content in the books. Still others work with Crisp Learning to customize the material to meet their specific needs and reflect their culture. Regardless of how it is used, we hope you will join the more than 20 million satisfied learners worldwide who have completed a *Fifty-Minute Book*.

Preface

This book lays a solid foundation for developing successful mentor behaviors. It enables the reader to identify and assess his or her own mentoring experiences—as mentor or mentee—and to use mentoring as an empowering tool for positive employee and personal development. The book deals with the practical aspects of mentoring, such as what makes mentoring special, assessing what the mentor is able and willing to invest in the relationship, and the special opportunities and challenges of cross-cultural, cross-gender, and supervisor-employee mentoring.

The how-to sections of the book deal with understanding mentee needs, positive mentor behaviors, behaviors to avoid, and ways to make the most of the mentor/mentee relationship in the short and long run.

This publication can be used as an individual workbook for exploring mentoring, or as a series of exercises to supplement a course on mentoring. Many of the exercises provide a basis for classroom or small-group discussion.

Gordon F. Shea

Gordon F. Shea

Contents

men•tor / ˈmen-ˌto(ə)r, ˈment-ər / *n* [L, fr. Gk *Mentor*] **1** *cap* : a friend of Odysseus entrusted with the education of Telemachus **2** : a trusted counselor or guide **3** : tutor, coach.

A new form of mentoring is evolving that is well suited to the downsized, high-tech, and globally competitive firms that have emerged in our society.

The concept of mentoring is no longer tailored to tall, hierarchical organizations. That old milieu was paternalistic and nurtured the status quo.

Mentoring is now seen as a process whereby mentor and mentee work together to discover and develop the mentee's latent abilities.

The goal is not a particular position within the company. Rather it is empowerment of the mentee by developing his or her abilities.

1

Mentoring As an Art

The Story of Mentor

The story of Mentor comes from Homer's *Odyssey*. When Odysseus, king of Ithaca, leaves to fight in the Trojan War, he entrusts the care of his household to Mentor, who serves as teacher and overseer of Odysseus' son, Telemachus.

After the war, Odysseus is condemned to wander vainly for 10 years in his attempt to return home. In time, Telemachus, now grown, goes in search of his father. Athena, Goddess of War and patroness of the arts and industry, assumes the form of Mentor and accompanies Telemachus on his quest.

Eventually, father and son are reunited and together they cast down would-be usurpers of Odysseus' throne and of Telemachus' birthright. In time, the word mentor became synonymous with trusted advisor, friend, teacher, and wise person. History offers many examples of helpful mentoring relationships, such as Socrates and Plato, Haydn and Beethoven, and Freud and Jung.

Mentoring is a fundamental form of human development where one person invests time, energy, and personal know-how assisting the growth and ability of another person.

History and legend record the deeds of princes and kings, but in a democracy each of us also has a birthright, which is *to be all that we can be*. Mentors are the special people in our lives who, through their deeds and work, help us to move toward fulfilling that potential.

HAVE YOU BEEN MENTORED?

Consider for a moment the following three questions regarding important changes in your life. In answering them, do not focus on the external events. Concentrate on the developments or changes that occurred within you—the way you saw yourself, others, or events.

1. Who provided an "aha!" experience that allowed you to pierce the core of the meaning of some event, in someone, in something, or in yourself? Write about one such experience in the space below:

   _____

   _____

   _____

2. Who provided you with a quote that had great meaning for you, that influenced your thinking or behavior, and that you sometimes repeat? Write down one such quotable quote and where it came from:

   _____

   _____

   _____

3. Who helped you uncover an aspect, an ability, or a talent of yours that, until then, had lain dormant and unrecognized? Describe one such incident:

   _____

   _____

   _____

Helping Agents

Mentors are helpers. Their styles may range from that of a persistent encourager who helps someone build self-confidence to that of a stern taskmaster who teaches a "student" to appreciate excellence in performance. Whatever their style, they care about their mentees and what they are trying to do.

You can learn much about mentoring from studying those who have affected your life and the lives of others. Mentor's job was not merely to raise Telemachus, but to develop him for the responsibilities he would assume in his lifetime. Mentors still pursue a similar task.

Mentoring is one of the broadest methods of encouraging human growth. Today, mentoring is often related to careers, but mentors can touch every facet of a person's being if their offerings are accepted and applied in diverse aspects to an individual's life.

It is impossible to divorce our career aspirations from aspects of our development as human beings, citizens, and members of our employing organization. To gain from mentoring, a person has to reach out, grasp, and draw into himself or herself the lessons that mentors offer. The mentee can only experience the beneficial gifts of mentoring by assuming ownership of what the mentor has offered and using it when appropriate throughout his or her life.

FROM LEGEND TO CHALLENGE

Mentors are people who have had a special or memorably helpful effect on our lives or inside ourselves. In each of the areas listed below, write the name of one person who had such an influence on you. Code the person's name if you wish, or use only a first name. If you cannot think of a person for a given area, go on and come back to that item later if someone occurs to you.

Mentors make important contributions to our...	**Someone who has been an influence or contributor for me...**
Knowledge of how societal systems, processes, or things work	_____
Values	_____
Technical competence	_____
Character growth	_____
Knowledge of how to behave in a social situation	_____
Understanding of the world about us	_____
Understanding of how to get things done in or through our organization	_____
Moral development	_____
Mental and physical health and fitness	_____
Understanding of other people and their viewpoints	_____
Other: _____	_____

New Visions

Traditionally, mentoring was a formal process whereby an older, more experienced person helped and guided a younger person in learning the ropes within an organization. Mentoring described the activities of a senior person preparing a junior for a particular office or job, providing career guidance, and encouraging high performance standards. When successful, mentoring had an important and beneficial effect on a person's career and life.

Mentors also were senior people in an organization who took talented young people under their wing and protected, taught, and even sponsored these protégés. However, in recent years this sponsoring role has been criticized for leading to favoritism, career climbing, and internal politics. In today's globally competitive organizations, many people dislike the word protégé and prefer the more neutral "mentee."

The traditional career-orientation definition of mentoring, while important, is seen as too limiting today.

You may be, or may become, involved in a formal mentoring relationship, as designated by your organization or undertaken as a voluntary activity. There are many opportunities to practice spontaneous or informal mentoring. Such relationships can be short or long.

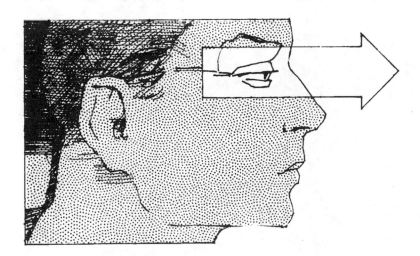

Mentoring's Many Forms

Mentoring can be defined as a significant, long-term, beneficial effect on a person's life or style, generally as a result of personal, one-on-one contact. A mentor is one who offers knowledge, insight, perspective, or wisdom that is especially useful to the other person.

Mentoring can be done by anyone, at any time, in almost any place. Mentoring can take the form of a one-shot intervention or a lifelong relationship. It can be carried out informally as an element of friendship, or formally as part of a highly structured employee orientation program. People who have been mentored often recognize that something very special has happened, but they may not even know what to call the experience.

Mentoring is a process whereby mentor and mentee work together to discover and develop the mentee's latent abilities and to encourage the mentee to acquire knowledge and skills as opportunities and needs arise. The mentor serves as an effective tutor, counselor, friend, and foil who enables the mentee to sharpen skills and hone her or his thinking.

Mentoring also can happen almost unconsciously. Someone may do or say something that will have an important effect on someone else. Or the recipient may become only slowly aware of how important a given intervention has been in his or her life. Yet these empowering links are not just beneficial accidents. Their power springs from the giving nature of the mentor and the receptiveness of the mentee to absorb, digest, and use the lessons passed to her or him.

Probably we have all had such experiences, both as mentor and as mentee.

A Variety of Mentoring Relationships

Describe one relationship you have experienced, observed, or known about for each of the four categories shown below:

Highly Structured

Formality of Relationship

1. **Highly structured, short-term.** The relationship is formally established for an introductory or short period, often to meet specific organization objectives. For example, a new employee may be paired with a senior person for company orientation.

2. **Highly structured, long-term.** Often used for succession planning, this relationship involves grooming someone to take over a departing person's job or function or to master a craft.

3. **Informal, short-term.** This type of off-the-cuff mentoring ranges from one-shot or spontaneous help to occasional or as-needed counseling. There may be no ongoing relationship. This type of intervention is often thought through and heavily change-oriented.

4. **Informal, long-term.** "Friendship mentoring" consists of being available as needed to discuss problems, to listen, or to share special knowledge.

Virtually No Structure

Short-Term Spontaneous ⟶ **Long-Term Even for Life**

Length of Intervention

A POTENT LIFE EXPERIENCE

In his autobiography, *Confessions of an S.O.B.* (Doubleday, 1989), Allen Neuharth, founder of the *USA Today* newspaper, tells a poignant story about mentoring.

Neuharth had moved to Detroit to be an assistant to Lee Hill, executive editor of the *Detroit Free Press*. Shortly after his arrival Neuharth was invited to lunch by Jack Knight, owner of the Knight-Rider newspaper chain, of which the *Detroit Free Press* is a part. They went to the posh Detroit Club where they had a cocktail. Then Jack Knight said, "Let's go."

A surprised Neuharth said, "Aren't we going to have lunch?"

Knight said, "Yeah, let's go."

Al was led six blocks to the basement lunch counter in the old Woolworth Five and Dime store. There, Jack Knight ordered a hot dog and coke and asked Neuharth what he wanted. Al had the same. Here was an immaculately dressed multimillionaire, a Pulitzer Prize-winning writer, and one of America's most powerful media moguls, handing Al a hot dog with mustard and ketchup.

Knight then said, in effect, "Lee Hill will give you memberships in the Detroit Club and the Athletic Club and take you to meet the mayor and a lot of other civic leaders, and after a while you will think you are writing for them. But remember, a lot of people who buy our papers eat here every day. Ask them what they read. Remember," Knight continued, "don't become a captive of your own comfort. Keep your feet on the street. And don't eat at the Detroit Club every day."

Neuharth relates that experience to the thinking that, years later, went into the creation of *USA Today* as a popular national tabloid.

This type of powerful life experience is what mentoring is all about. Mentors provide exceptional learning experiences for their mentees and highlight key ideas and information that make events memorable and meaningful. They expand their mentees' awareness, insight, and perspective. Mentors can be a powerful force for developing employees and enriching organizations. Mentoring experiences often contain a bit of improvisation and drama, which we later remember and use.

SHARING LIFE EXPERIENCE

Write your answers in the spaces provided.

1. Has anyone ever arranged an unusual learning experience for you that allowed you to see into another sphere of life or to look behind the scenes? Describe one such episode.

_____

_____

_____

2. Describe the most unusual mentoring experience you have encountered, and indicate its importance to you.

_____

_____

_____

3. Identify one situation where you provided an unusual experience for another person, which opened new vistas for them, enabled them to see how other people live, or helped them see something important in a new light.

_____

_____

_____

Mentors Are Special Helpers

Even formal mentoring is largely the art of making the most of a given situation. This flexible view tends to distress some individuals, who expect and perhaps need a cookbook approach to every task. They want to know exactly what they are supposed to do, how to do it, and when to do it.

Learning that mentoring is part intuition, part feelings and part hunch—made up as you go along, and composed of whatever ingredients you have available at the moment—is too uncertain for some people. But that is largely what it is, and it derives its power from that reality.

For example, a person who learns counseling skills can become a counselor and perhaps a mentor. But mentoring occurs only when the counselor creates an intervention in the relationship that goes beyond counseling; otherwise, the word mentoring has no special meaning. Helping an employee cope with a mate's alcoholism is not necessarily mentoring—it is more like counseling. But even a casual remark, if it reveals a new facet of a problem, can be mentoring, whether it is made by a counselor or anyone else.

This special spark, which reveals new aspects of things in a flash, is often missing in today's education and training. Fortunately, people other than educators and trainers often provide it. These are people who care enough about a person to make it happen. Mentoring goes beyond what we learn in schools.

Why are today's organizational leaders so interested in promoting a type of relationship that is so amorphous and random? Because in an increasingly complex and high-tech environment we all experience a need for special insight, understanding, and information that are outside the normal channels or training programs. There may be people around us who can help fill in cracks in our comprehension of the complex problems we face. These special people are our mentors.

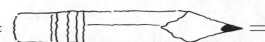

IDENTIFYING OUR LIFE HELPERS

Identify three people who have significantly and beneficially influenced you. Describe what they have contributed to your life:

1. Someone who has inspired you to shift the direction of your life in a constructive way.

2. Someone who has provided something to help you grow in depth of feeling, character, moral or ethical integrity, or who has helped you develop a deeper commitment to your values.

3. Someone who has provided some form of help to you at *just the right time*.

Were any of these assists a spontaneous response to a great need of yours—whether you had recognized the need at the time or not? If so, which?

WHAT MENTORS DO

Following is a list of things that mentors do. As appropriate for each one, check "Others have done this for me" or "I've done this for others" (or both).

Mentors...	Others have done this for me	I've done this for others
Set high performance expectations	❏	❏
Offer challenging ideas	❏	❏
Help build self-confidence	❏	❏
Encourage professional behavior	❏	❏
Offer friendship	❏	❏
Confront negative behaviors and attitudes	❏	❏
Listen to personal problems	❏	❏
Teach by example	❏	❏
Provide growth experiences	❏	❏
Offer quotable quotes	❏	❏
Explain how the organization works	❏	❏
Help far beyond their duties or obligations	❏	❏
Stand by their mentees in critical situations	❏	❏
Offer wise counsel	❏	❏
Encourage winning behavior	❏	❏
Trigger self-awareness	❏	❏
Inspire to excellence	❏	❏
Share critical knowledge	❏	❏
Offer encouragement	❏	❏
Assist with careers	❏	❏

The Extra Mile

Except in formal mentoring programs where a mentor is assigned to guide a mentee, a mentoring relationship is not duty bound. Teachers who dispense information under contract or lawyers who tender counsel for a fee are merely doing their jobs. Mentoring is more than doing a job—it is help that goes beyond obligatory relationships.

Teachers can mentor and so can lawyers. The difference between a teacher and a great teacher is often due to the extra mentoring component that some people offer. Most of us have known many good and competent teachers who do their work with art and style. The fortunate ones among us also have encountered teachers who have fired a spark within us, who opened new vistas and dimensions before us, who touched us deeply and who awakened and encouraged our potential.

Similarly, a senior lawyer might take a young person fresh from the bar exam under his or her wing. The senior lawyer might teach the novice the ropes of the legal profession, call on the mentee to meet the most exacting professional standards, and provide encouragement and comfort during the tough period of getting one's feet on the ground in a law firm.

Mentoring requires going above and beyond. It is a relationship in which a person with greater experience, expertise, and wisdom counsels, teaches, guides, and helps another person to develop both personally and professionally to meet exceptional standards of performance.

But what of the senior person in an organization who has been *assigned* the task of mentoring a junior person in a formal mentoring program? If that person performs his duties in a perfunctory fashion, the essence of the experience will be missed for both mentor and mentee.

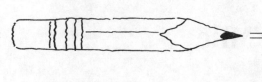

REACHING OUT TO ANOTHER PERSON

Mentoring is often the extra increment of help that makes a truly important difference to a mentee.

Relate an experience where you reached out to another person who was deeply in need, and your help appeared to make a significant beneficial and perhaps long-lasting difference to that person.

_____

_____

_____

Describe one experience you observed, read, or heard about where someone reached out to another person to help in an unusual way. It need not be as dramatic as the Neuharth story, but it often has an imaginative or unusual twist to it that helped make the experience memorable and of continuing utility to the receiver.

_____

_____

_____

Describe one mentoring experience you have had which did not fit the direct, one-on-one personal aspect of mentoring. For example, a special parental message, a quote from literature, a speech, a sermon, etc.

_____

_____

_____

Is Mentoring

for You?

Investing in Others

Are you ready, willing, and able to mentor others? Are you emotionally and psychologically prepared to invest time and effort in helping another person? Do you have the time, skills, and freedom to devote yourself to another person? Are you ready to make such a commitment?

To mentor is to change your life, if only in small ways. Impromptu, off-the-cuff mentoring requires at least a heightened awareness of the needs of others and a willingness to pause or listen for a while. Taking on a formal mentoring assignment at work may mean occasional inconveniences and less time for other duties. Mentoring a young person as a community effort can conflict with family commitments and personal activities. Mentoring can mean substantial personal change—perhaps a willingness to listen more and talk less, for example.

Mentoring that causes you significant stress or loss in other areas should be weighed carefully before you make a commitment. Yet, if you are ready, the personal satisfaction may be well worth the time and effort expended—"eyes open" are the watchwords.

Mentors also need to believe in the value of their work without worrying about returned favors. If you have, or can develop, a freely giving nature, you probably will mentor all through your life—probably without thinking much about it.

Your Investment in Mentoring

Mentoring can range from a spur-of-the-moment intervention to an intense long-term relationship. The mentee's needs and the mentor's resources vary over time, reflecting the complexities of life, and it is important to assess where you are at the moment. Conditions and interests need to be reappraised from time to time.

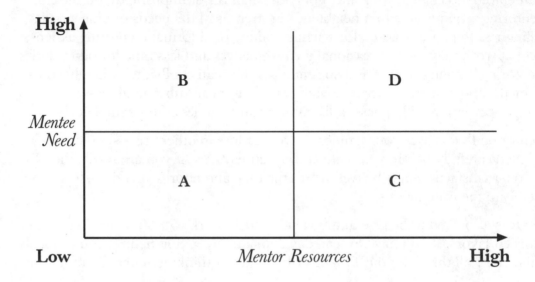

Quadrant A: The mentor's resources and mentee's needs are low, spontaneous, or occasional. Very short-term interventions may be adequate and satisfying to both parties.

Quadrant B: The mentee's need is high and the mentor's resources, time, skills, etc., are low. Helping the mentee find a more appropriate mentor or professional help may be appropriate.

Quadrant C: The mentor's resources are substantial, but the mentee's needs are low. Occasional help may be all that is needed, and the mentor may have time and talent available for helping others.

Quadrant D: The mentee's need is high and the mentor's resources are abundant. The potential exists for an intense and productive relationship.

The mentor and mentee's willingness, readiness, and appropriateness need to be judged according to the individual situation. A very willing mentor trying to work with a mentee who perceives little need for help is inappropriate. Similarly, a needy mentee and an overloaded mentor may not work well together.

SHARING RESOURCES

Mentors bring a variety of resources to a mentoring event or situation. These vary according to the mentor's job, personality, interests, experiences, network of friends and associates, and available time and energy. In the spaces below, identify the special assets that you bring to a mentoring situation. List one or more items in each category.

My position or work experience:

_____

_____

Things I like to do:

_____

_____

My education, training, and/or experience:

_____

_____

My pastimes, hobbies, and/or clubs:

_____

_____

My special skills and knowledge:

_____

_____

My special passions:

_____

_____

Any other assets:

_____

_____

The Empowering Mentor

Sound mentoring respects the uniqueness of the mentee and strives to enhance the special strengths of that person. Effective mentors tend to focus on *what* the mentee does in response to the mentor's help rather than *how* he or she does it. Barring some negative or destructive response that could harm the mentee or others, mentors need to focus on the positive results of a transaction—if they are visible.

The desire to "do it my way" is critical to a mentee's sense of self, for it respects that person's specialness. Doing something the mentor's way may lessen the mentee's sense of ownership. It may also be a way for the mentee to avoid thought or responsibility. It also may be downright uncomfortable for the mentee. The mentee should adapt the mentor's help to his or her own situation and style. This enables the mentee to wrestle with the details, perhaps try different approaches, and discover personal talents or strengths.

Because mentees may choose to do something their own way and not appear to do what was expected, mentors may not recognize that their mentoring has been effective. An effective mentor lets go or, more importantly, does not take charge of the mentee. A helping relationship is a freeing relationship. A mentee's success largely hinges on him or her designing a personal blueprint for how to proceed.

NON-DIRECTIVE WAYS OF MENTORING

Identify three situations where you have served or could serve as an effective role model.

1. _____

2. _____

3. _____

Identify two positive attitudes you display, and two ways you help others to overcome negative feelings about themselves.

Positive attitudes:

1. _____

2. _____

Helping others:

1. _____

2. _____

How comfortable do you feel just listening to people with problems?

_____

_____

People seldom want to be told what they should do or how to do it, but an idea or a bit of information offered in a neutral way becomes something they can identify and use. Assess your own ability to share ideas and information in a neutral context.

_____

_____

Mentor Self-Development

Some of the best mentors are people who assume that they, as well as their mentees, are in a lifelong process of self-development. Long ago, or so it seems, a person could develop a certain level of wisdom and sophistication and pass this knowledge on to those younger and/or less experienced. But now our world changes each day. Therefore, it is necessary to decide what types of mentoring can be practiced most successfully and what knowledge and skills are needed to develop to stay up-to-date.

➤ **Focus on basic principles and fundamental truths.** This may not be a static activity. Applying fundamental truths to new challenges requires constant reassessment, discussion, and even argument until new wisdom is forged. Supreme Court justices, ecclesiastics, and good supervisors do this.

➤ **Keep abreast of new developments and their implications.** This is a more dynamic source of mentoring. It means that a mentor's task of self-development, learning, and mastery is never finished. This need not be a heavy task if the mentor chooses specialties such as the evolving mission of an organization or the technology in a given field.

➤ **Mentoring is an evolving field.** If, as a mentor, you choose to master active listening, coaching skills, effective confrontation techniques, or new methods of resolving conflict, you are starting a journey of self-development.

MENTORING STYLES

There is a need to match mentoring styles to the personalities involved, and to develop your own knowledge, skills, and abilities in ways that are compatible with your personality.

Do you like to philosophize, discuss, and argue interesting points?

_____

What is your response to mentoring from a thoughtful viewpoint?

_____

_____

Do you like to be active, interested in what works, and get things moving?

_____

What is your response to mentoring that relies on action or example?

_____

_____

The above questions are a simplified way to encourage you to think about mentor and mentee styles. What type of mentee would you work with most productively?

_____

_____

_____

List three types of self-development you might consider to become the type of mentor you would like to be.

1. _____

2. _____

3. _____

CASE STUDY: IKA

Ika is a streetwise young man in his late teens. He lives in a tough inner-city neighborhood with his mother and two younger brothers. He dropped out of high school, but after a bout with drugs and rehabilitation he managed to earn his high school equivalency diploma. Last fall he started taking two evening courses at a community college. He passed both courses with marginal grades, and signed up for two more this semester.

You are the supervisor of a shipping department and Ika's boss. You have noticed that Ika learns quickly, works steadily, is careful with the equipment and merchandise, and occasionally asks penetrating questions about how things are done. He has made several good suggestions about work methods, which you implemented. You suspect he has several types of talent.

You live in a pleasant suburban neighborhood, belong to the local American Legion Post, coach a boys' softball team, serve as a vestryman in your church, and spend the rest of your free time with your family. You have 14 years with the company.

Your company plans to automate the materials-handling system in the plant and the shipping department. You have been asked to recommend one employee who knows the present system to serve as a liaison person. That person will work with the consultants who are to study the system and develop changes. Jim, the most experienced person, plans to retire soon. Ika knows the system well enough, but he would have to be coached on some details. The three other employees are not good candidates. Two are fairly new and the other skips work fairly often.

Last week Ika said his studies were getting him down and wondered aloud whether he had what it takes to graduate from college. He said one of his teachers loads students down with homework and does not explain things clearly. He is also discouraged about ever being able to get his family out of "that neighborhood."

CONSIDER IKA'S CASE

What risks might be involved in mentoring Ika?

_____

_____

If you decide to get involved with Ika, what might you plan to do?

_____

_____

Considering all the commitments you have, the nature of your work, and the demands of the new project, would you be willing to mentor Ika on a serious level?

_____

_____

If you decided to spend more time helping Ika, what other aspects of your life and work might you consider changing?

_____

_____

What difference does it make if Ika is African American and you are Caucasian?

_____

_____

What difference does it make if Ika is Caucasian and you are African American?

_____

_____

Compare your responses to the author's comments in the Appendix.

Understanding

Mentees' Needs

Adapting to Change

All mentees will have some general needs that they share with others from a similar background or situation. They also have a personal and unique agenda and individual values, perceived limitations, and aspirations. Complicating this highly personal equation is guidance from a mentor and other opinions, desires, and events that intrude upon a mentee's daily life.

In mentoring, the mentee is called upon to consider changes suggested by his or her mentor. The changes may be generated by a challenging opportunity or through a personal insight. For mentees, change is the name of the game, whether it is self-imposed, a new option, or intrusive.

Managing this change takes place in a constantly shifting personal and organizational environment. There is bound to be a sense of loss from giving up familiar and comfortable beliefs, behaviors, and even relationships. There is fear of the unknown and of possible failure, even when those feelings are willfully suppressed. Ironically, there may be anxiety when success is achieved–people may fear that they will not measure up to the expectations placed on them by themselves and others because of that success.

A part of a mentor's role is often simply to be there for the mentee, to listen, to comfort, to be a friend.

The mentor's challenge is to recognize the needs of a person adapting to change and to respond appropriately.

READING MENTEE SIGNALS

Problem messages from a mentee usually contain a fact and a feeling. "Jack, I've got a financial problem that just won't let go of me" is a factual statement of a person's perception. But it doesn't clearly emphasize a feeling. List three factual statements a mentee might make to signal that he or she is experiencing a problem.

1. _____
2. _____
3. _____

Some problem messages focus on a feeling that is complicating the person's problem-solving ability. "My financial condition is driving me crazy" signals the stress the speaker is suffering. List three *feeling* statements a mentee might make.

1. _____
2. _____
3. _____

Feelings also can be expressed nonverbally through facial expressions, tone of voice, gestures, or posture. List three nonverbal ways a mentee might signal a feeling.

1. _____
2. _____
3. _____

These feelings are important. They should not be discounted. Statements such as "don't worry about it," "it can't be that bad," or the cheerful "everything will turn out all right" demonstrate that you are not taking a mentee's problem or the mentee seriously.

Fostering Positive Self-Image

All people have a need for confidence and a positive self-image. How individuals respond to problems almost always reflects that their feelings about themselves at that time or their general perception of self. Research indicates that two-thirds of the population suffers from generalized low self-esteem. They have negative feelings about aspects of themselves or attributes they possess.

This focus on one's deficiencies makes it difficult to feel energetic, to be motivated, or to make positive changes. A mentor's primary role is to provide genuine confidence-building insights and experiences.

A less appreciated means of damaging one's self-image is the way the mentee talks to or about himself. Virtually everyone carries on an inner dialogue. This inner-conversation can be negative if it focuses on failure or shortcomings. Many of us, in fact, have been taught to depreciate our achievements rather than revel in them. This pulls down our spirits and sense of achievement. Is it any surprise that so few of us make much use of our inherent talents? It is one thing to suffer a defeat and feel discouraged but quite another to beat yourself up over it.

A mentor can:

➤ Listen to the discouragement without passing judgment, thereby giving the mentee a chance to vent negative feelings.

➤ Provide ideas for remedy when asked.

➤ Offer help (as the mentee needs it) once the person has decided on a problem-solving course of action.

BUILDING SELF-CONFIDENCE

Allowing and encouraging a mentee to talk through negative feelings enables the person to move beyond those feelings. List three specific responses you might make to negative comments that would keep the ball in the mentee's court.

1. _____

2. _____

3. _____

Considering your resources such as position, experience, and contacts, identify three things you might offer to expand a mentee's horizons and/or build personal confidence.

1. _____

2. _____

3. _____

Suggest three ideas that could help your mentee build a more positive self-image.

1. _____

2. _____

3. _____

How can you and your mentee increase the number and quality of your mutual life-enhancing experiences?

1. _____

2. _____

3. _____

Managing Change

When a person is undergoing significant change, five things are necessary to adapt successfully to the change:

➤ A clear vision of how the mentee and his or her situation will be after the change

➤ Time to absorb the new vision

➤ Time to adjust behaviors

➤ Coping mechanisms to manage the stress of change

➤ Time to ponder the meaning of the change, and to internalize and own the change

Context shifting is key to this process. People are more likely to do things that move them toward a goal if they can clearly imagine what their world will be like after the change is successfully accomplished. This mental adjustment needs to be imagined in positive terms, not in the dread scenarios we often create in our minds. Helping mentees shift their mental context from today's problems to tomorrow's successes can be very productive.

Don't expect instant change. In fact, quick change can be so stressful as to be overwhelming or encourage backsliding.

Mentees need healthy coping mechanisms to deal with the stress of change. Mentors help mentees expand their range of positive coping mechanisms and avoid counterproductive ones, such as drinking alcohol when the going gets rough.

Example: A laid-off steelworker who thinks of himself as only a laid-off steelworker may block other options, get discouraged, and turn to drink or drugs. A mentor who helps the mentee envision and become comfortable with alternate futures, such as computer programming, will help that person to consider pursuing serious alternatives.

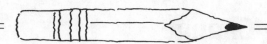

MEETING MENTEE NEEDS

Think of one valuable change that you would like to make in your life. Imagine what you and your environment would be like if you accomplished that change. Focus on positives. Describe this change:

_____

_____

List three ways you bolster your own self-image:

1. _____

2. _____

3. _____

Identify three ways you use time to adapt to necessary or desired change (an example is developing new skills or knowledge):

1. _____

2. _____

3. _____

List three effective coping methods you use to deal with stress in your life:

1. _____

2. _____

3. _____

Which of these techniques are you willing to share with a mentee?

Cross out any unhealthy or negative coping mechanisms listed above. You would not want to pass these on to a mentee.

Dealing with Gray Areas

Helping someone to grow as a person is not always straightforward or simple. Mentees have their own lives, with a variety of demands from a variety of sources, and they change daily in a multitude of ways. Every day we each grow older, meet new people, encounter new problems and challenges, and perhaps suffer some defeats. No matter how little we seem to change, remaining the same is impossible.

Some mentee adaptations may not be dramatic or even noticeable. They may be gradual and almost imperceptible. Some may be cloaked.

If the mentoring relationship is long-term, the mentor may need to:

➤ Pick up on subtle concerns the other person articulates

➤ Notice small or gradual changes that seem significant

➤ Read verbal and nonverbal signals

These concerns, changes, and signals can become response points. Such signals can be clues that help is needed. They may even help to bring the problem to the surface of the mentee's awareness or to define an emerging difficulty.

SETTING MUTUAL PARAMETERS

Dealing effectively with small problems to keep them from becoming large ones is a primary way mentors can assist their mentees.

Identify three verbal or nonverbal clues that a mentee might give, perhaps unconsciously, that suggest that he or she is having job or career problems:

1. _____

2. _____

3. _____

Identify three repetitive patterns that might indicate an individual is experiencing difficulty in his or her personal life:

1. _____

2. _____

3. _____

Identify three repetitive complaints from a mentee that might indicate an unresolved personal difficulty, such as being frequently victimized by others:

1. _____

2. _____

3. _____

Listen for the use of absolutes such as "I *never* seem to get along with my bosses," or "He gets to me *every* time we have a conversation." Stated absolutes seem accurate to the holder, but may or may not be valid. However, acknowledging and discussing them can be a good starting point for identifying and addressing a problem.

CASE STUDY: PAM

Pam is a very bright and sparkling person you met in the company cafeteria. She works for Harold Greening in Accounts Payable.

You served as an informal mentor to Pam on three or four occasions in the last few weeks when she wanted to talk about a problem she has with her finances. You listened, were nondirective in your responses, and gave her information when she asked for it. She said you were very helpful. She also solved her financial problem in a clever way that never occurred to you.

You have learned that Pam graduated from high school and has a certificate in secretarial sciences from a local business school. She seems well-trained, but not well-educated. Her perspective on the world is limited, as is her experience. Yet she seems fascinated with the variety and challenges inherent in your job. Her grasp of the difference between your work and lifestyle and hers has led her to talk about changing her life to one that is more challenging and diverse.

You have heard that she is a hard worker and quick to catch on. You believe she is capable of great things, but she seems unaware of her natural intelligence and abilities. This comes out in her conversation when she discounts compliments about her intelligence and ability. She says she is dumb, but everything she does belies that assertion.

You believe that if her self-image and self-confidence were to rise, her talents would become obvious.

CONSIDER PAM'S CASE

If you decide to continue informally mentoring Pam, what special aspects of mentoring would you emphasize?

_____

_____

Would your mentoring be affected if you were a male? How?

_____

_____

How would you attempt to make Pam more aware of her special abilities and talents?

_____

_____

Could focusing on positive self-talk be helpful to Pam? If so, how would you convey the concept and its importance to Pam?

_____

_____

The change Pam is considering would be substantial, extremely varied, and would take a long time to complete. How could you help?

_____

_____

Compare your responses to the author's comments in the Appendix.

Positive Behaviors

Seven Types of Mentor Assistance

Research has revealed seven types of assistance a mentor can provide that are particularly helpful in encouraging mentee development. They are:

1. **Shifting context.** Help a mentee envision a positive future or outcome.

2. **Listening.** Be a sounding board when a mentee has a problem.

3. **Identifying feelings.** Feelings can motivate mentees to achieve success or set themselves up for failure.

4. **Productive confrontation.** Discuss negative intentions or behaviors without being judgmental.

5. **Providing appropriate information.** Suggest possible solutions or sources of helpful information.

6. **Delegating authority and giving permission.** Empower a mentee's self-confidence and counteract negative injunctions that defeat success.

7. **Encouraging exploration of options.** Help mentee's consider possibilities beyond the obvious or "tried and true."

These seven items can do much to encourage mentees' personal growth. Their strength lies not in a notion that they meet all of the needs of a mentee—they don't, but when offered at important junctures in a person's life they can help the person resolve a problem, make a decision, or move on.

Shifting Context

Imagination is a critical component of personal development. You've heard the expression, "if you can imagine it, you can be it." Your mentee may need help imagining an alternate reality to the present. Constructive imagination is an important component for success in any field or endeavor. By contrast, a gloomy outlook toward one's future often precedes failure.

As a mentor, if you help mentees create a satisfying new vision for their life or work, mentees will do most of what is necessary to bring the vision to reality.

The art of personal transformation often happens at a subconscious level—people see themselves receiving a promotion, for example, and begin to do the things that will guarantee success. Creating a personal concept of what success would look like, sound like, feel like, and even taste like, can be a motivation toward positive goal achievement. Successful people use this type of mental stimulus to guide them on their path to where they want to be.

But some people get stuck. They rely on outmoded visions and habits. They say "because I never finished college, I will never be promoted to manager." As the world moves ahead, they wallow in obsolescence and possibly despair. A vision of achieving a managerial level, however, might inspire them to take night classes and finish college.

Mentors can help their mentees envision worthy goals and move toward their fulfillment.

CASE STUDY: CARL

Carl Ditton had worked as an engineer for 15 years, designing microcomputer circuits for an electronics firm. He was rated as a success and made good money. But he was bored out of his mind and wanted out.

One day when he was meditating, he envisioned himself selling large beautiful homes to various people. He was excited by the image. He drew up a list of conditions that would be necessary for him to succeed in real estate sales. This was not a plan-he would rely on his creative subconscious to lay out a plan he could follow intuitively. Yet he knew he had the prerequisites: He worked well with people, and was articulate, organized, and persistent.

Later, Carl used his list of conditions to imagine himself as a successful real estate agent selling large, beautiful homes to a host of people, and earning generous commissions. He imagined his family enjoying a spacious new home, which they owned outright.

He soon found himself signing up for a course basic to get his real estate license. Ten years later he was a multi-millionaire, enjoying his work enormously. Carl believed that the secret to his success was envisioning himself in his new role. He worked at vividly seeing, hearing, and feeling himself working as a successful real estate agent. He could even smell the flowers in the garden of the home he imagined himself selling.

Envision one personal goal you would like to achieve—something that is actually possible, rather than, say, becoming a rock star though you have no musical training. Picture yourself being there. Focus on the *what*, not the *how*. Describe what it will be like when you achieve it:

_____

_____

Now, consider using this same type of envisioning exercise with your mentee to help him or her shift context to a positive future focus.

Listening

Have you ever wished you had someone to talk to about things that were bothering you? How many times have you experienced the therapeutic relief of being able to get something off your chest by talking it out?

Mentees benefit from the same experience. *Respectful listening* is probably the most powerful activity a mentor can bestow. Respectful listening means providing an ear without taking on the other person's problems, giving advice, or joining them in the "ain't it awful" game.

Respectful listening is the ability to become absorbed in what another person is saying about a problem, treating that person's words as confidential communication, and not injecting your own subjective views, opinions, or suggestions. This gives the other person an opportunity to gain insight into a problem by articulating it, to sort things out, perhaps to develop a solution, and almost always to gain emotional release and relief.

Respectful listening means allowing your mentee to talk without interruption and accepting that what is being said is genuine, at least to the speaker. Listening to another person for that person's sake is not a discussion. You also listen during a discussion, but during active listening your role is to help another person unload their troubles.

Identifying Feelings

When your mentee is speaking, listen to the words said, but also listen for the underlying feelings. In problem messages, feelings are usually more important than facts and are paramount as motivators. The facts are the objective reality; how a person feels about those facts usually identifies whether or not a problem truly exists, the dimensions of the problem, and its level of importance.

For instance, "What time is it?" asked in a matter-of-fact voice reflects a need for information. The same question phrased as "Heavens, what time is it?" and asked with urgency is quite a different message—it indicates a potential problem. The objective reality (the time of day) may be the same in both cases, but the expressed urgency in the second situation implies a need for action.

Unfortunately, the emphasis our society places on facts often diminishes our capacity to recognize other people's feelings and perhaps even our own. Yet feelings are important because they motivate our actions—and an inability to detect feelings can cause us to miss the most important part of the message someone is sending.

Listening for Motivation

Researchers who study motivation tell us that there are four basic emotions: *fear*, *anger*, *grief*, and *joy*. These range in intensity from a little to a lot. Fear may range from a vague uneasiness to panic; anger may be felt as a minor annoyance or as uncontrolled rage. Responses to these emotions also vary. Fear or grief can be so deeply repressed that there is virtually no response until the emotion becomes overwhelming.

Emotions are often combined with thoughts, which leads to feelings such as disappointment, embarrassment, and satisfaction.

The capacity to detect the emotions and feelings of others and to respond appropriately is a critical art of mentoring. Since feelings motivate people to do or not do things, overlooking them can limit a mentor's effectiveness. Below are several statements a mentee might make. Identify the feelings and the motivations they might induce.

Mentee Statement	Feeling Expressed	Motivation	Likely Action
It seems like a good idea...but I just don't know.	Ambivalence—finds idea attractive, yet is afraid.	To delay or avoid.	Little, late, or none.
I just heard our company has filed for bankruptcy!			
Can you believe it? My supervisor just chewed me out in front of everyone.			
This assignment opens the door to a great future for me.			
I don't think I'll make it in this program. I'm so far behind.			

LISTENING FOR FEELINGS

Below are three statements that might be made by a mentee. Listen for the mentee's underlying emotional message.

1. "When I first joined this organization, I really thought I was going to get somewhere. Well it's been two years now and I'm still doing the same old thing." Write your perception of this message:

   _____

   _____

2. "This is the type of work I can really sink my teeth into. I get so wrapped up in it I forget when to go home. Sometimes I lie awake nights thinking about it." What message is the mentee sending?

   _____

   _____

3. "When I made that presentation on Tuesday, I thought you'd support my position. Instead you only sat there. You didn't open your mouth once. What's a mentor for anyway?" What message is the mentee sending?

   _____

   _____

Identify the feelings the mentee is expressing in each statement:

   1. _____

   2. _____

   3. _____

Productive Confrontation

Sometimes a mentor will have to confront a mentee's attitude, behavior, or plans if they are destructive or negative. Yet criticizing, threatening, or pressuring the mentee to adopt another course can lower the mentee's self-esteem. Criticism also can be ineffective, causing the mentee to retreat from the relationship.

Communications specialists find that confrontation is less threatening if it is phrased as an "I" message—an authentic message directly from the mentor—rather than a "you" message. A "you" message may sound like a put-down: "You are going about this all wrong."

An "I" message generally contains three parts:

1. A neutral description of what you perceive the mentee intends to do.

2. A statement of the possible negative effects on the mentee or other people.

3. The feelings or emotions you have about the mentee's plan.

An I message works because it does not tell the mentee how to behave. The mentee makes the decision.

Example:

Your mentee has stated, with determination, her intention to tell off a supervisor in another department.

The subsequent conversation might look like this:

Mentor: *"I'm concerned that you are going to blast Joe, because such an encounter could damage your relationship with his department."*

Mentee: *"I don't care, he's got it coming."*

Mentor: *"Now I'm concerned that you want to go ahead without regard to the consequences."*

After an I message is sent, the receiver often shifts to a somewhat different tack; follow with a modified I message if that happens, rather than repeat the same message.

Also, if the receiver changes to a more constructive approach, you might change to active listening and reflective feedback.

"I" MESSAGES

Write an appropriate I message for each of the three situations described below.

1. Your mentee has made a derogatory remark about a co-worker's ethnic, cultural, or racial origins.

   _____

   _____

2. Your mentee says mentoring does not seem to be helping him and he wants to drop the relationship.

   _____

   _____

3. Your mentee is working full-time and has family obligations as well. She says she wants to sign up for several college courses in the fall. You are concerned that the overload could lead to failure and, consequently, discouragement.

   _____

   _____

Look at your I messages again. Do they contain:

➤ A clear but neutral statement of the problem as you see it?

➤ A statement of the negative consequences that you believe would follow from the mentee's action?

➤ A statement of your feelings or concerns about the mentee's behavior or intention?

CASE STUDY: RAY

You are Imelda Rodriguez, a highly successful account executive who has, over the last five years, consistently generated the highest earnings for your division. Three months ago you were asked to participate in a formal mentoring program for newly hired recent college graduates. You were assigned to mentor Ray Golightly during his first six months on the job.

Ray strikes you as hell-bent on getting to the top as soon as possible. You find nothing wrong with his ambition—it resembles your own. But you question some of his methods.

Ray seems to devote most of his time and energy to making connections rather than demonstrating his abilities through performance.

Ray refers to work assignments from his supervisor as "busy work." He turns in "hastily performed, somewhat sloppy work," to quote his supervisor.

Your company was downsized three years ago and several layers of management were eliminated in the process. The organization is now lean and mean with everyone carrying a heavy load. When you explained this to Ray, he saw an opportunity. "Fewer people to get in my way," he responded. He continued to behave as before.

Ray played up to you at first, but then interpreted your efforts to help him as "getting on my case."

It would be easy to not recommend Ray for retention—and to warn him of your intention. But as his appointed mentor, you feel you should make a greater effort to salvage him. You are not quite sure how to go about it.

CONSIDER RAY'S CASE

Could Ray's perceptions of corporate life be based on feature movies about corporate climbing? Considering the company's downsizing, could Ray's notions be out-of-date? Give your views.

_____

_____

_____

_____

What mental model does Ray probably have of corporate life? List three or more components of his probable model:

_____

_____

_____

_____

From the concepts and tools discussed in this chapter, develop a plan for mentoring Ray. Outline your plan:

_____

_____

_____

_____

Is internal competition or internal cooperation likely to offer the greatest rewards in our increasingly professional, highly technical society? Explain your view:

_____

_____

_____

_____

Compare your responses to the author's comments in the Appendix.

Providing Appropriate Information

It is always a mentee's responsibility to instigate changes in their lives. As a mentor, your job is to listen, and sometimes confront inappropriate decisions. It is also appropriate to occasionally provide information that a mentee can use to guide his decision-making process.

Information that is neutral and factual can empower a mentee or be stored away for future use. Be aware, however, that opinions and advice are subjective and may be more valued by the giver than the receiver.

When a person with a problem is ready to resolve the problem, a mentor can provide relevant information, while still leaving responsibility for solving the problem to its owner. Sometimes a mentor can point the way to useful information, letting the mentee do his or her own research.

Delegating Authority and Giving Permission

Good supervisors, managers, and executives do not really "delegate" tasks, jobs or projects. They assign them. To delegate means to give someone a job to do but without relinquishing responsibility for it. However, if someone is assigned to do a task because they have the necessary knowledge, skills, and abilities, they also should be empowered to make key decisions related to the project.

Handing authority to another person indicates a significant level of trust and confidence in their ability. This kind of trust can have a positive and long-lasting effect on a mentee's development. As a mentor, you can help bolster your mentee's self-confidence by giving him a responsibility and only checking in for progress reports now and then, rather than overseeing every detail yourself.

Giving permission is another valuable aspect of mentoring. The training your mentee received as a child may impede resolution of certain problems. For example, you may encounter a mentee who harbors a deep-seated fear of enjoying her work, achieving recognition, or earning too much money. You might need to act as a counterweight to earlier inhibiting messages, letting the mentee know that it's okay to strive to win, take risks, strategize, change course, be smarter than the next person, and so on.

Use caution, however. Don't push a reluctant person too hard, but carefully listen as he talks—sometimes in a roundabout way—about his injunctions and difficulties he has trying to overcoming them.

Encouraging Exploration of Options

People often box themselves in by "either/or" thinking, becoming so emotional that "they can't think," or relying on "tried and true" answers. First, listen to get to the core of the mentee's issue or difficulty. Then you may suggest that together you brainstorm solutions or different actions. However, be conscious of becoming too enamored with one option or another—it is the mentee who has to choose a path and make it work.

GROWTH INFLUENCES

Answer the questions below that you feel comfortable answering.

Is it time for a change? There are times in life when an individual's personal growth may begin to strain a given situation, as when a teen hungers to become an adult.

Identify three situations where a mentee might be ready to move on to a new stage of development.

1. _____

2. _____

3. _____

Think back to an important decision you had to make in your own life where you were torn between alternatives. List three things you needed from those close to you.

1. _____

2. _____

3. _____

Think back in your life to a point where you made, or were about to make, a serious mistake or error in judgment. Identify three things that someone else did or could have done to keep that situation from turning out badly.

1. _____

2. _____

3. _____

Consider which of these situations an effective mentor could have influenced for the better. What could such a person have done to help you?

_____

_____

PART 5

Behaviors to Avoid

Avoiding Negative Behavior

Mentors want good things to happen to their mentees. They want them to be effective, productive, achieving, successful, and happy. However, in their eagerness to help their mentees, they may revert to behaviors that are less than helpful. Three such behaviors are:

> ➤ **Criticizing**

> ➤ **Giving advice**

> ➤ **Rescuing people from a self-inflicted folly**

Dr. Eric Berne was a psychiatrist and the father of transactional analysis—a method for analyzing human communication to determine its psychological content and intent. He pointed out that the three behaviors listed here are components of negative psychological games that involve put-downs of another person, you, or everyone in general. Such games are unhealthy. Someone, or everyone, comes out of the game feeling badly—angry, depressed, or fearful.

Such psychological games often begin with an absolute statement such as "John, you are always late, you're *never* on time." These grandiose exaggerations trigger rejection of the message, resistance, and argument. So John's actual behavior—the fact that he's late today—does not get examined or dealt with. These psychological games tend to become endlessly repetitive. The nag continues to nag, the person being nagged resists, and little change in behavior occurs.

Most of us have been taught, at least by example, to criticize, give advice, and rescue people inappropriately. Research on mentoring skills indicates that these behaviors should be avoided.

CONSTRUCTIVE ALTERNATIVES

Do you enjoy or seek criticism? When you ask for feedback, do you secretly hope for some favorable information?

List five things another person could do to help you change for the better. Consider personal examples such as losing weight, stopping smoking, etc. Think about how another person could really help you.

1. _____

2. _____

3. _____

4. _____

5. _____

What causes you to feel best when you are making progress toward a significant personal goal? List five things that help your progress.

1. _____

2. _____

3. _____

4. _____

5. _____

When you try something and get in trouble as a result, how do you want people close to you to behave? List five behaviors you would like.

1. _____

2. _____

3. _____

4. _____

5. _____

Remember the ideas you listed here when you're working with a mentee. What works for you will probably work with others, too.

The Problem with Criticism

Have you noticed how most people do not take kindly to criticism, even when it is offered as "constructive criticism"?

No matter how we sugarcoat it, criticism is evaluative and judgmental. We offer "constructive" criticism because we want our message to be helpful to the other person. But our intentions are undercut by the way that criticism damages self-esteem, generates defensive blocking, and drains the energy needed for constructive action. Also, accepting criticism entails acknowledging that a behavior was bad or wrong—something a mentee is unlikely to do if the action was intentional.

The two most powerful human motivators are survival and security. Criticism and evaluation threaten these motivators. For some people, criticizing, complaining, and nagging only tends to prolong the problem. Ever notice how little change results from nagging?

Avoiding criticism does not mean accepting negative behaviors, performance failures, or self-defeating repetitive actions. When a mentee's behavior is not up to snuff, it's important to think through an effective intervention.

The key to success is not to repeat ourselves endlessly and negatively, as critics tend to do, but to take new, objective, and creative approaches to encouraging beneficial change. When a person's performance is not up to standard, the person may need information rather than criticism.

Healthy Alternatives

What are the "thinking" alternatives to criticism? Mentors are most beneficial when they help their mentees break out of negative behavior patterns. When a person makes the same mistake repeatedly, the solution is not to give the same answer over and over again. The most positive route to change is to look at the transactions and identify the repetitive elements so they can be changed—even if the change is painful.

For example, if a mentee repeatedly fails on the job, instead of merely encouraging the person to do better, complaining, or issuing warnings about the consequences, analyze the problem to find the underlying cause.

A performance failure can be viewed as the "gap" between what is needed and what is produced. This gap needs to be described and measured. A mutual plan needs to be developed for closing the gap so that the problem disappears. Mentor and mentee need to cooperate in problem solving.

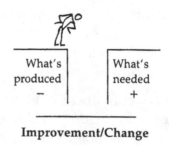

The performance gap is described in neutral terms that are specific and measurable, often suggesting, by implication, a way to solve the problem.

Evaluative vs. Neutral Terms

Think of three personal or performance problems you have encountered. Describe them first in evaluative terms, then in neutral terms that are specific and measurable.

Evaluative Terms	**Neutral Terms**
Your reports are always late.	Your last three reports were each 2–3 days late.
1. _____	_____
_____	_____
2. _____	_____
_____	_____
3. _____	_____
_____	_____

The Problem with Advice

Many mentors believe that a large part of their job is giving advice.

There is a downside to giving advice, because it assumes that the advice-giver has superior knowledge, insight, or wisdom. This may be true in professional discourse.

But when the issue is a mentee's personal problem, whether job related or not, the mentee is likely to know more about the problem than the mentor ever will. After all, he or she has been living it. Advice or suggestions about personal problems is often countered with frustrating resistance and a lot of "yes, buts." This should not be too surprising. It is presumptuous and even a little arrogant to assume to know more about another person's problems than that person does.

You can serve your mentee best by:

➤ Listening carefully.

➤ Feeding back the emotions that are expressed to demonstrate that you understood the deeper, emotional nature of the difficulty.

➤ Providing ideas or information when asked, which the mentee can use to help weave a solution.

Most independent-minded mentees do not really want advice, though they will value your experience, ideas, knowledge of how things work, and special insights into problems. To respect their independence, offer but do not push. They must learn to make their own decisions, if they have not already.

Effective mentors stick with helping, not interfering. They share, they model, they teach; they do not take over someone else's problems unless there is a crisis that requires immediate action. Mentee growth depends on the mentee taking responsibility for solving his or her problems.

Information vs. Advice

Dr. Steven B. Karpman devised the Drama Triangle as a way of analyzing psychological games. It illustrates why people often resist taking advice.

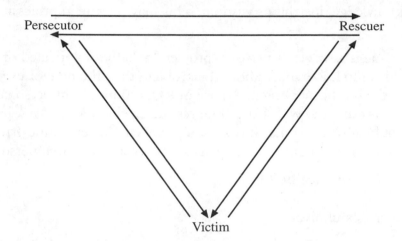

Someone who feels victimized by a problem may send a plea of "help" to another person who is perceived as a rescuer (i.e., a more capable person). The victim's feelings of inadequacy are real, but his lack of ability usually is not.

The would-be rescuer accepts the inadequacy of the victim and offers advice. In doing so, she contributes the "why don't you" component to the "why don't you—yes, but" psychological game.

Most often the victim rejects the advice with "yes, but," followed by a reason for not taking the advice. This is hardly surprising, since the person knows all of the facets of the problem and has probably already considered and rejected the easy answers.

The rescuer has only the information that the victim gives in response to each suggestion. Each new suggestion is rejected for some seemingly new reason.

Finally, the rescuer grows impatient with the rejections and turns persecutor, responding with something to the effect of, "Buzz off—you don't really want to solve this problem."

At that point, each party is confined in his or her own judgment. The victim feels even more like a victim. He not only still has the original problem, he also has to deal with the would-be rescuer who is exasperated with him. The would-be rescuer has confirmation that that the victim was and still is inadequate. The victim is convinced that the problem is too big to be solved by anyone. And the relationship has been damaged.

The Problem with Rescuing

The world is full of genuine victims, people who, through no fault of their own, come upon hard times, as when a hurricane strikes, or there is an auto accident, or an employer goes out of business. These people need help.

Another type of victim also needs help, but of a different type of help. Some individuals, because of feelings of inadequacy, prior victimization, or poor adaptation to a crisis, set up repetitive patterns of failure. Most of us do this in some areas of our lives. If we never experienced actual failure, we would fail to achieve all that we are capable of.

When dysfunctional behavior patterns occur in a mentee's personal or work life, a mentor can help by pointing out the repetitive nature of the transactions. The mentor can use counseling skills to help the mentee break the pattern.

Rescuing the mentee, or attempting to take over the problem is not likely to be helpful in the long run. Temporary help in a crisis may be appropriate, but when there is a recurring pattern of such rescuing, the mentor becomes part of the mentee's problem.

MISDIRECTED HELP

Mentoring should be a pleasant, satisfying experience. When we get annoyed, suspicious, or anxious, our negative feelings are clues that something is amiss. They signal a need for problem identification, definition, and resolution. In each of the following mentee statements, identify the feelings to help define the nature and magnitude of the problem. Then identify an ineffective, but typical, intervention or response. Then indicate a constructive response based on material in this manual.

Example: "I'm worried about what you told me to do about the Owens case. If it goes badly my whole career will be up for grabs."

Feeling: Very scared, possibly angry that his or her career is being discounted.

Typical Intervention: "Don't worry about a thing, I wouldn't have suggested it if there was any possibility of it going wrong."

Effective Response: "You seem very concerned about the consequences. Let's talk about it in detail. I want to hear exactly what is troubling you."

1. "I think the intern program is a waste of time. It isn't doing me any good and I want to drop out of it."

   Feeling: _____

   Typical Intervention: _____

   Effective Response: _____

2. "Once again I thought I had a chance to really make it, and once again I've failed."

   Feeling: _____

   Typical Intervention: _____

   Effective Response: _____

3. "It seems like I can never get ahead. My finances are a mess, I've got bill collectors after me all the time, and I just don't know what to do. I may even face bankruptcy."

   Feeling: _____

   Typical Intervention: _____

   Effective Response: _____

CASE STUDY: EDDY

Eddy Chang recently graduated from a first-class engineering school. He joined your department less than a year ago. He is amiable and well liked by his co-workers. His engineering qualifications are impressive.

You are Jim Backus, his technical supervisor. You are the lead designer and have been with the organization 12 years. You have spent considerable time teaching Eddy as much as you could, but there is a language barrier. You have a hard time understanding his speech and he sometimes seems to have trouble understanding yours.

Eddy's family migrated here from Southeast Asia several years ago. Relatives sponsored his family in the United States, and Eddy completed most of high school and college here with good marks.

By working very hard at it, Eddy can adequately present his ideas in writing, but his verbal presentations are disastrous. His presentation to an in-house weekly symposium bombed. His slides were overloaded with equations, he mumbled as he read his notes, he failed to look at his audience, and he presented his verbal information in a sketchy, abbreviated fashion.

Some of the participants dozed, some read other materials, and a few in the back talked among themselves. During the question-and-answer time, not one question was raised. You were embarrassed both for Eddy and for your colleagues and their behavior.

Later your manager asked you to mentor Eddy as well as supervise him. Since you were teaching him the work as fast and as well as you could, you thought you had been mentoring. When you pointed this out, your boss said, "No, this goes beyond doing your job. Try to be a friend to him, help him to succeed. Do what you can to turn him into a winner."

CONSIDER EDDY'S CASE

List what you see as Eddy's obstacles to success:

_____

_____

What cross-cultural problems might be lurking?

_____

_____

List some ideas as to how you might help Eddy.

_____

_____

Compare your responses to the author's comments in the Appendix.

Mentor-Mentee

Gains

Developing a Partnership

Mentoring is sometimes perceived as a one-way street, with the mentor giving and the mentee receiving. This top-down, parent-to-child view of the relationship is often based on the assumption that the mentee is not in a position to do much in return except be a dutiful and appreciative protégé.

This idea is especially prevalent in organizations where the mentor is a senior person and the mentee is a junior. It is difficult to engage in adult-to-adult communication even though the mentee is an adult. This reinforces the giver-receiver aspect of the relationship. The senior/junior relationship seems so natural that few people question the assumptions on which it was based.

In the past, this limitation often worked, giving career success to the mentee and a type of parental satisfaction to the mentor. But it tends to produce clones and prepare people to succeed in a world that is now passing. In these days of self-empowerment and rapid organizational and professional change, the senior-junior model needs revision.

Today, mentoring should be viewed as a partnership with both parties freely contributing to the discussion as equals working together with mutual respect. A mentor may still have greater experience, insight, and wisdom, but the relationship can be one of sharing (even material sharing) rather than only top-down giving and receiving. After all, the mentor *helps* but the mentee *does*—or the relationship is a failure.

Making the Most of the Relationship

Mentoring is not a bookkeeping exercise. There is no need to balance accounts or to give back in kind. Yet a two-way flow of kindness, respect, or giving can return much to the mentor. In the spaces below, explore ways that giving can flow freely in the relationship.

From the mentor's perspective: *Things you would like to get from the relationship—candor is critical here.*	**From the mentee's perspective:** *Things a mentee could contribute to the relationship.*

Anticipated Gains

As a cultural value, we extol selfless generosity. We give for love—of our mate, our children, our parents, and our neighbors. This giving is usually honest and sincere. But since we also have needs, we hope that others will apply the golden rule and that some joy will come our way. If it does not, we may be disappointed and possibly resentful.

Acknowledging that each of us has needs and being open and honest about them can help make our expectations explicit. Failing to state our expectations of another person is all too common and unfair. Mentees and mentors need to be explicit about what they hope to gain from the relationship. This helps both parties determine if the match is likely to be a good one.

ASSESSING PERSONAL EXPECTATIONS

As a mentor, what do you hope to get in return for your investment in time and effort?

1. Types of satisfactions:

_____

_____

2. Types of recognition and from whom:

_____

_____

3. Types of rewards:

_____

_____

4. Other benefits or returns:

_____

_____

5. Would you be willing to share these hopes or expectations with your mentee? If not, why not?

_____

_____

Determining Mentee Expectations

A few mentoring relationships end badly: in anger, in quarrelling, or in disappointment. As with nasty divorces, these traumatic partings often result from unmet expectations on one or on both sides. Some expectations may be buried deeply in a person's culture or upbringing, such as perceptions of what a man is supposed to do or what a woman is supposed to be like. Expectations may be subconscious and never surface until a quarrel erupts.

For example, in recent years many firms have downsized their operations and laid off large numbers of midlevel managers and professional workers. Several stories have appeared in print with people complaining that their mentors failed to take care of them. "When the going got rough, he worried more about his own career than he did about mine," complained one young professional.

It is unlikely that the mentors and mentees ever discussed whose career came first. Yet some mentees had that expectation and levied it against their mentors without having made the assumption explicit. If the mentees had been called protégés and told that their mentors would be responsible for their career advancement, the assumptions might make sense.

Efforts should be made to address mentee expectations before the relationship begins, during mentee training, in exploratory talks between mentor and mentee, and through small-group discussion. Mentor expectations should be similarly developed or expressed—at least during mentor training—and openly shared with the mentees.

Checking Mentee Expectations

Three methods of ascertaining mentee expectations are:

➤ Ask the mentee to write a brief essay describing what he or she expects to gain from the relationship—short-term and long-term.

➤ Ask the mentee to briefly identify his or her perception of the roles and responsibilities of each party in the relationship.

➤ Ask the mentee to list any special needs or features of the relationship that should be considered in developing the relationship.

It is important that the mentor not overreact to the mentee's expectations. They are usually an honest statement of expectations derived from the mentee's background and his or her notions about what mentoring is. If the mentee's expectations are more than the mentor is willing to accept, they should be negotiated.

Developing a Mentor-Mentee Agreement

A mentor-mentee agreement may be helpful when an employer, school, or other agency establishes a formal mentoring program.

When both parties to a mentoring relationship have made their expectations clear, a reconciliation of views may be necessary. At least they should define how they will work together and what they hope to achieve through the association.

The agreement need not be formal or even written down. Any effort to set up a potential "I gotcha" situation is unhealthy. Mentoring is, at its foundation, a friendly, helping, informal relationship; any effort to extract promises is probably based on fear, mistrust, or hostility.

The goal of the agreement is to set objectives for a mutual effort. It is a tentative agreement, subject to change as required. It is mutual in that both parties should benefit in satisfaction and happiness.

From the days of the medieval craft guilds to today's apprenticeships and training programs, there have been agreements between mentors and their mentees. Some are written, most are not. Whether written or verbal, what each person is willing and able to initially invest in the relationship should be worked out and agreed upon, as well as what outcomes are expected. The greatest value in developing such an agreement and making it explicit comes from the freewheeling discussion between mentee and mentor. An accepting demeanor is essential in these discussions.

TESTING A MENTOR-MENTEE AGREEMENT

In formal mentoring, every agreement has key points that indicate how well it is working.

Examples of key points:

Mentee will complete next computer course as part of her Individual Development Plan

Mentee will join Toastmasters and attend monthly meetings to improve speaking skills

Mentee will develop a list of agenda items to discuss during weekly meetings

Depending on the nature of the agreement, these key points should be checked periodically. Mentor and mentee should discuss points that need to be amended, dropped, or improved. One system that works well entails a 30-day checkup, a 90-day review, and a six-month examination, which can be repeated every six months indefinitely. Of course, any problem should be dealt with when it arises.

What are three key points that a mentoring agreement might contain?

1. _____

2. _____

3. _____

How might these key points be adjusted in a 30-day checkup?

1. _____

2. _____

3. _____

CONTINUED

CONTINUED

In a 90-day review?

1. _____

2. _____

3. _____

In a six-month examination?

1. _____

2. _____

3. _____

CASE STUDY: MARY JANE

Mary Jane is 72 and hasn't missed a day of work in more than 30 years. She is cheerful and helpful to everyone, performs well, and says she expects to be around until she's a 110. Mary Jane thrives on hard work. She participates in several civic and charitable activities and takes one college course a semester—usually in a professional subject, but occasionally she signs up for a "fun course." Pictures of her grandchildren and great-grandchildren adorn her office.

Recently, Ellen Kuhary announced she will retire in seven months. The next day Mary Jane asked you to help her prepare to apply for Ellen's job. She is amply qualified and has the seniority—though seniority here is more a custom than a rule. She noted that you have successfully mentored several women, and though you are not in Ellen's chain-of-command you know a lot about her work that would be helpful.

You are a corporate vice president, the most successful woman in the corporation. You have broken many historical taboos about women's careers. You could provide unique insight into Ellen's job and its relationship to the work of other departments. However, Kurt Smith, Ellen's supervisor, doesn't take kindly to other people's involvement in his area.

Mary Jane has told Kurt she is interested in Ellen's job. He was surprised and commented on her age. She shot back that his remark could be the basis of an age-discrimination suit, but that she wanted to win the job by her proven ability and her record. She reportedly left Smith gasping for breath. The Federal Age Discrimination in Employment Act and a state law allow Mary Jane to continue working indefinitely, as long as her performance is up to standard.

Mary Jane also told Ellen she wanted to be her successor. She said, "Succeeding in your job would be the crowning feather in my career cap." Ellen likes Mary Jane and is probably mentoring her. However, Mary Jane has told you clearly that she wants to "earn that job."

CONSIDER MARY JANE'S CASE

In light of the politics, should you agree to mentor Mary Jane?

_____

_____

What would you be willing to offer Mary Jane as your mentee? List as many items as possible.

_____

_____

Would actively listening to Mary Jane in detail be appropriate here?

_____

_____

Identify any items that should be part of a mentoring agreement you might make with Mary Jane.

_____

_____

What personal rewards might you derive from mentoring Mary Jane?

_____

_____

Compare your responses to the author's comments in the Appendix.

Special Situations

Mentoring and Changing Demographics

Mentoring can be applied to a variety of people, situations, and purposes. In academic settings, mentoring is used to stimulate and motivate gifted students, to acclimate new students to college life and its challenges, and to provide help by older students to younger students in specific subjects. Government agencies provide technical mentors to recently graduated new hires in professional fields, assign mentors to personnel just entering the executive ranks, and train senior personnel as mentors to facilitate an agency's adjustment to increased workforce diversity. Private firms use mentoring as an instrument for organizational development (not just as a career development tool), as a method for adapting the organization to competitive challenges, and for succession planning.

Informal mentoring also takes a wide variety of forms and serves a host of mentee needs. In-country mentors help international businesspeople adapt to unfamiliar cultures, mores, and legal codes. And the list of applications is growing.

The three special mentoring situations described in this chapter—cross-gender, cross-cultural, and supervisor or manager mentoring—are examples of sensitive situations where mentoring can have dramatic, positive results. They represent three primary challenges when mentoring is used to adapt a workforce to demographic changes already underway, to prepare for operation in a competitive global environment, and to manage organizational and technological change effectively.

IDENTIFYING SPECIAL ISSUES

Now that you are familiar with the many ramifications of mentoring, list 10 areas in your organization where formal or informal mentoring could be helpful.

1. _____   6. _____
2. _____   7. _____
3. _____   8. _____
4. _____   9. _____
5. _____   10. _____

Consider how competition, changes in your organization's mission, or other external factors affect the future of your organization. Identify 10 trends that could have an impact on you and other employees.

1. _____   6. _____
2. _____   7. _____
3. _____   8. _____
4. _____   9. _____
5. _____   10. _____

Identify three ways in which mentoring might be used to influence the organization's future and that of the people within it.

1. _____

_____

2. _____

_____

3. _____

_____

Cross-Gender Mentoring

Until recently, cross-gender mentoring in organizations has been rare. Several mentoring studies revealed a number of problems related to cross-gender mentoring due to gossip, envy, suspicion, speculation, false assumptions, sexual stereotypes, and charges of sexual harassment. Unfortunately, such attitudes and behaviors lessen the effectiveness of cross-gender mentoring in some environments. Yet each sex has much to offer and teach the other. Cross-gender mentoring can leaven the workplace, enrich the lives of mentees, and provide valuable insights and experiences to each sex.

A gender-balanced and fairly treated workforce is likely to remain a challenge rather than a reality for some time. Effective cross-gender mentoring as a tool might help bring about this balance and fairness.

INSIGHTS THROUGH BALANCE

List five advantages to the organization or to society from cross-gender mentoring:

1. _____
2. _____
3. _____
4. _____
5. _____

If you were to mentor someone of the opposite gender, what unique skills might you offer?

1. _____
2. _____
3. _____
4. _____
5. _____

If you were to mentor someone of the opposite gender, what unique skills might you learn?

1. _____
2. _____
3. _____
4. _____
5. _____

Cross-Cultural Mentoring

Look around. Signs of cultural diversity are everywhere. This diversity represents some of the most subtle and special relationships imaginable. Even in relatively homogeneous societies, differences in economic class, religious background, regional allegiance, and even family traditions can generate cultural differences that complicate the task of mentoring.

Cultural differences and our response to them are part of what makes each of us unique. Our cultural uniqueness also may enable us to appreciate special facets of a problem, approach its solution from different angles, and contribute to a more comprehensive, elegant, and lasting solution. As we move from a society of things to one of human values, mentoring offers a powerful tool for benefiting from cultural diversity. By carefully listening, by respecting differences, and by practicing the art of inclusion, we can build a stronger, more rewarding organization and society.

Identifying Cross-Cultural Contributions

When you go to a restaurant, attend church, listen to music, watch a movie, go to work, speak to another person, play games, dance, or receive medical treatment, you enjoy advantages based on the diverse contributions of people from all over the world. We can trace the origin of a plate of spaghetti to China, modern medicine to ancient Arabia, the roots of Christianity to Hebrew tribes, modern dance rhythms to Africa, or the Tex-Mex meal we just enjoyed to the ancient Toltecs of Mexico. Our lives have gained richness and variety from people all over the world, whether we are aware of it or not. The contributions are endlessly varied.

Can You Think of Some Cross-Cultural Contributions?

Identify five ways in which different cultures currently contribute to society.

1. _____

_____

2. _____

_____

3. _____

_____

4. _____

_____

5. _____

_____

Mentoring by a Supervisor or Manager

Some of the most powerful, effective, and long-lasting mentoring can be done by the person who has authority over a mentee—and this can include parents. The power or authority to reward and punish people creates both opportunities and obstacles to effective mentoring.

The possession of authority over a mentee can work against a helping, caring, nurturing relationship. It is difficult for a mentee to become personally responsible when subjected to pressures from others.

Yet power and authority need not be negative. When used wisely to challenge, to offer opportunities, and to encourage, power and authority can provide a mentee with powerful assistance. The mentor can model proper use of personal power—through voice, writing skills, and persuasion. The power of expertise and the power of judgment provide valuable learning opportunities for a mentee.

Mentoring by a supervisor or manager must be done carefully, artfully, and fairly. If you mentor subordinates, mentor all of them. In one respect, bringing out the best in each employee may well define the meaning of supervision. Mentoring can contribute strongly to the development of that art.

The Issue of Hierarchy

Hierarchy is not simply a matter of placing people on an organizational ladder. There are hierarchies of knowledge, of experience, of seniority, and of position and power. Hierarchies of influence, personal complexities, and abstraction also exist.

List three ways you, or someone you know of, are able to influence others through avenues that are not related to layers of organizational structure:

1. _____

2. _____

3. _____

MENTORING BY SETTING AN EXAMPLE

Rank has an obvious relationship to hierarchy. But rank can blind us to more subtle relationships in mentoring. Identify one or more people you respect and admire who rank highly in your estimation because of the example they set in the following areas:

Integrity: _____

Sensitivity to others: _____

Consideration of others: _____

Moral or ethical leadership: _____

Loyalty: _____

Any other area: _____

Write down three ways you can use your power or influence to help a mentee—whether you thought of that person as a mentee or not—to broaden his or her horizons, experience reasonable challenges, or understand a special facet of his or her work or activity:

1. _____

_____

2. _____

_____

3. _____

_____

A P P E N D I X

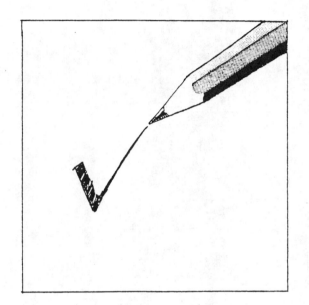

Author's Comments on the Case Studies

Case Study: Ika (page 27)

Ika sounds like an ideal individual to mentor. He has an overriding clear-cut goal—to "get his family out of that neighborhood." He is carrying out a plan (college) for achieving his goal. Also, after dropping out of school and a bout with drugs, he has made an excellent comeback—getting his high school equivalency diploma. Ika has considerable potential.

It is clear that Ika is an excellent choice to work with the consultants. He will learn a great deal in helping to set up the new system, and his discussions with you will benefit you both.

You might ask yourself:

> ➤ How can I ensure that Ika continues to work steadily, is careful with the equipment and merchandise, asks penetrating questions, and is recognized for those characteristics?

> ➤ How can I encourage Ika to continue to contribute workable suggestions?

> ➤ How can I discover and bring out more of Ika's talents?

> ➤ Can I find tutoring help for Ika in his current studies and in his career planning?

Since your mentoring is likely to occur on the job, much of the differences in lifestyle and interests are background material, and may only be useful in helping you both to understand each other's viewpoints.

Case Study: Pam (page 40)

Pam is like so many underdeveloped gems in every workplace. Like many of us, she needs to go on a voyage of inner exploration, discovery, and conquest. She needs to shed many of her images about herself, open up to the world around her, and learn to live the more interesting and varied life she desires.

However, it is critical that Pam find her own path and establish her own milestones as she progresses through life. She may believe she wants to be "just like you," but that would probably be a delusion and possibly counterproductive.

Every human being is unique, and though we may learn from one or more role models, the problems Pam will encounter, the opportunities that arise for her, and the time and environment in which she will achieve her goals, will be her own—and must be respected as such.

It is important to encourage her rather than impress her. Discuss doable, worthwhile, and interesting things that appeal to her. Note that pushing a person tends to create pressure and resistance. Also, if you carry most of the weight for Pam, she will be less likely to experience her own inner sense of achievement.

Find out what she likes to do, what she is interested in, and how she spends her non-working time. Ask open-ended questions such as: Do you like to travel? What kind of activities do you enjoy most? You are trying to help Pam find her authentic self.

Since this is informal or spontaneous mentoring without any particular goals except to help Pam realize her full potential, take your time and play it by ear.

Case Study: Ray (page 53)

Ray seems like the mentee from hell—the one most likely to try a mentor's soul—yours perhaps. The irony may be that Ray might become a valuable employee. There are some reasons why he is acting the way he is and you might be able to help him. You may want to try the "I" message approach with Ray:

➤ Start with a neutral, factual, or unbiased "description" of his behavior, such as "You refer to your supervisor's assignments as 'busy work' and your supervisor says you turn in 'hastily performed, somewhat sloppy work.'" That may not sound neutral or unbiased, but it is as close as you can get under the circumstances, and it is a factual description of what you know.

➤ Add a statement of the negative effects of Ray's behavior on Ray, his supervisor, or other people: "It affects your supervisor's output," and "Can hurt work group morale because they have to pick up the slack," or, "It could adversely affect your supervisor's performance review."

➤ Explain your feelings or emotions about his behavior: "As a concerned member of this organization and as your mentor, your behavior troubles me."

Remember, do not tell Ray how to behave—he must learn this on his own. Also, do not threaten or pressure him—that enables him to justify his resistance. He needs to understand that his performance review will depend upon his behavior.

For the "I" message, focus on the most important issues—the ones he can do the most about. Ray can't change the past, but he can change his future behavior and his work habits.

Case Study: Eddy (page 70)

Your supervisor is asking you to rise above supervisor, teacher, and coach and add the extra dimension of mentor to the relationship. To be a "friend," to "help him succeed," to "do what you can to turn him into a winner." These are all awesome goals with great rewards.

Keep up the teaching, tutoring, and supervising that you have been doing with Eddy, but be alert for opportunities to go above and beyond those activities. What clues are there?

➤ He graduated from a first-class engineering school

➤ He is amiable and well-liked by his co-workers

➤ His engineering qualifications are impressive—try to figure out his strengths

What are the difficulties?

➤ Understanding his speech

➤ He has trouble with verbal presentations

➤ He mumbles as he reads his notes and doesn't look at his audience when he gives his presentations

➤ His slides are overloaded

There are elocution teachers who perhaps can help him clarify his speech and presentations—find out what can be done with company support. Could his tendency to mumble and not look directly at his audience be a cultural trait? You may need to discuss Eddy's issues with some expert helpers. The problem may be far more complex and subtle than you realize.

Case Study: Mary Jane (page 82)

Mary Jane is a treasure to her organization. Based on her past performance, she could continue to add considerable value to the organization for many years to come.

As her mentor you should explore your own attitudes, beliefs, and possibly stereotypes about her age, health, and personal contributions on the job.

If you get past those barriers successfully, you can probably relate well to other people who fall outside our traditional concepts of the ideal employee, such as the physically or mentally challenged, the bias against older employees which is fairly common, and all of the other differences that sometimes may block fairness toward an individual.

The great challenge today is to use all types of diversity to benefit your organization. Each human being is incredibly complex. Researchers are exploring new tools to understand and work cooperatively with people who are quite different from each other. In the decades to come, especially as more organizations and their employees "go global," these skills will become a necessity.

For instance, many organizations have used the Myers-Briggs Personality Preference Indicator to match mentors and mentees. This is an analysis that has no right or wrong answers. It tells you a great deal about how you prefer to act when given a choice. Each individual profile is considered right for each person. The exercise can be used to help each of us understand, appreciate, and work better with each other.

Mary Jane is an archetype of the increasingly common person who loves their work and their involvement in it. If it seems strange to have such a mentee, there will be a lot for you to learn as the workplace develops, but you will have lots of fun with your mentees.

Mentoring can be formal or informal. It's up to you! It can be a long- or short-term investment, a single action, or an agreed upon plan. The success of your relationship depends upon the commitment you and the mentee are willing to make to meet the challenges and capitalize on the opportunities.

The rewards are great and we hope this book has helped you identify the practical aspects of assessing, developing, and maintaining positive mentoring behavior.

Happy Mentoring!

Additional Reading

Bell, Chip R. *Managers as Mentors*. San Francisco, CA: Berret-Koehler Publishers, Inc., 1996.

Bonet, Diana. *The Business of Listening*. Menlo Park, CA: Crisp Publications, 2001.

Cook, Marshall J. *Effective Coaching*. New York, NY: McGraw-Hill, 1999.

Evans, Thomas W. *Mentors: Making a Difference in Our Public Schools*. Princeton, NJ: Peterson's Guides, 1992.

Goleman, Daniel. *Emotional Intelligence*. New York, NY: Bantam Books, 1995.

Hathaway, Patti. *Giving and Receiving Feedback*. Menlo Park, CA: Crisp Publications, 1998.

Kravitz, Michael and Susan Schubert. *Emotional Intelligence Works*. Menlo Park, CA: Crisp Publications, 2000.

Lloyd, Sam. *Self-Empowerment*. Menlo Park, CA: Crisp Publications, 2002.

Minor, Marianne. *Coaching and Counseling*. Menlo Park, CA: Crisp Publications, 2002.

Scott, Cynthia D. and Dennis T. Jaffe. *Managing Personal Change*. Menlo Park, CA: Crisp Publications, 1989.

Shea, Gordon. *Making the Most of Being Mentored*. Menlo Park, CA: Crisp Publications, 1999.

NOTES

CRISP WORLDWIDE DISTRIBUTION

English language books are distributed worldwide. Major international distributors include:

ASIA/PACIFIC

Australia/New Zealand: In Learning, PO Box 1051, Springwood QLD, Brisbane, Australia 4127   Tel: 61-7-3-841-2286, Facsimile: 61-7-3-841-1580
ATTN: Messrs. Richard/Robert Gordon

Malaysia, Philippines, Singapore: Epsys Pte Ltd., 540 Sims Ave #04-01, Sims Avenue Centre, 387603, Singapore   Tel: 65-747-1964, Facsimile: 65-747-0162 ATTN: Mr. Jack Chin

Hong Kong/Mainland China: Crisp Learning Solutions, 18/F Honest Motors Building 9-11 Leighton Rd., Causeway Bay, Hong Kong   Tel: 852-2915-7119, Facsimile: 852-2865-2815 ATTN: Ms. Grace Lee

Japan: Phoenix Associates, Believe Mita Bldg., 8th Floor 3-43-16 Shiba, Minato-ku, Tokyo 105-0014, Japan   Tel: 81-3-5427-6231, Facsimile: 81-3-5427-6232
ATTN: Mr. Peter Owans

CANADA

Crisp Learning Canada, 60 Briarwood Avenue, Mississauga, ON L5G 3N6 Canada
Tel: 905-274-5678, Facsimile: 905-278-2801
ATTN: Mr. Steve Connolly

EUROPEAN UNION

England: Flex Learning Media, Ltd., 9-15 Hitchin Street,
Baldock, Hertfordshire, SG7 6AL, England
Tel: 44-1-46-289-6000, Facsimile: 44-1-46-289-2417   ATTN: Mr. David Willetts

INDIA

Multi-Media HRD, Pvt. Ltd., National House, Floor 1
6 Tulloch Road, Appolo Bunder, Bombay, India 400-039
Tel: 91-22-204-2281, Facsimile: 91-22-283-6478
ATTN: Messrs. Ajay Aggarwal/ C.L. Aggarwal

SOUTH AMERICA

Mexico: Grupo Editorial Iberoamerica, Nebraska 199, Col. Napoles, 03810 Mexico, D.F.
Tel: 525-523-0994, Facsimile: 525-543-1173   ATTN: Señor Nicholas Grepe

SOUTH AFRICA

Bookstores: Alternative Books, PO Box 1345, Ferndale 2160, South Africa
Tel: 27-11-792-7730, Facsimile: 27-11-792-7787   ATTN: Mr. Vernon de Haas

Corporate: Learning Resources, P.O. Box 2806, Parklands, Johannesburg 2121, South Africa, Tel: 27-21-531-2923, Facsimile: 27-21-531-2944 ATTN: Mr. Ricky Robinson

MIDDLE EAST

Edutech Middle East, L.L.C., PO Box 52334, Dubai U.A.E.
Tel: 971-4-359-1222, Facsimile: 971-4-359-6500   ATTN: Mr. A.S.F. Karim